Original title:
Terracotta Tales

Copyright © 2025 Creative Arts Management OÜ
All rights reserved.

Author: Samuel Kensington
ISBN HARDBACK: 978-1-80581-835-9
ISBN PAPERBACK: 978-1-80581-362-0
ISBN EBOOK: 978-1-80581-835-9

Vibrant Shadows

In a garden of clay with figures so bright,
Gnomes dance in the moon, such a comical sight.
One trips on a root, lands right on his face,
Laughter erupts in this playful space.

Birds gossip above, gossip's such a delight,
A squirrel jumps down, says, "I won the fight!"
With a cap made of leaves, he struts all around,
In the land of the funny, silliness abound.

A hedgehog in glasses reads wise tales of old,
While a rabbit shows off his carrot-shaped gold.
Chasing shadows at dusk, the stories unfold,
Of giggles and blunders that never grow old.

The Alchemy of Earth

Once clay was a lump, now a llama in hats,
He strolls through the soil, befriends all the rats.
With a wink and a nod, he's the talk of the town,
In his kingdom of dirt, he wears a brown crown.

A wizard of mud brews his potions with glee,
Accidentally turns chickens to fish in the sea.
The townsfolk all chuckle, they can't get enough,
For a fish on a bicycle? Well, isn't that tough!

Each twist of the earth brings a laugh and a cheer,
As moles drop top hats, quite the style, I hear!
The alchemy of giggles, they flourish and grow,
In this quirky world where wild wonders flow.

Palette of the Past

With a brush made of roots, the past comes alive,
Shapes of earthen folks, oh how they thrive!
One roams with a scarf, all knitted with yarn,
While another spins tales, "Hey, my name is Barn!"

A painter, quite muddy, splashes joy all around,
With polka-dot mushrooms exploding the ground.
He mixes his colors with a cackle and snort,
Creating odd critters, Picasso would court!

As history giggles, it's hard not to smile,
Each creature's a story that stretches for miles.
In this palette of fun, colors burst in delight,
Painting laughter's rich hues, from day until night.

Earth's Storytellers

Gather 'round, dear friends, let the stories unfold,
 Of rocks that tell secrets, and dirt that is bold.
The wise old oak chuckles, "I've seen quite a lot,"
While a beetle debates if the moon's really hot!

 A ladybug chimes in, "But wait, there's more!"
"Let's discuss the time I flew right through a door!"
While a worm claims, "I've traveled the globe!"
 With tales intertwined, in laughter they probe.

As shadows grow long, under stars they conspire,
 Each tale more ridiculous, sparking their fire.
Earth's storytellers echo, in giggles and sighs,
 Creating a chorus of whimsical lies.

Relics of Time

Old pots are laughing, cracking jokes,
In a dusty museum, where no one pokes.
A vase winks slyly at a startled spoon,
"I bet I'm older than you, oh monsoon!"

Mismatched socks in a cabinet's corner,
Hiding from dust, a true soft-warner.
A teapot grins, "I brew stories galore,
Come sip on me while I croon evermore!"

Shapes in Clay

Lumpy, bumpy, a cheeky bowl,
"I'm not just a dish, I'm a playful soul!"
A puppet-like mug dances off the shelf,
Singing to mugs, "You must learn to be-elf!"

A few mugs chatter, "Have you seen the dish?
She dreams of grandeur, makes a wish!"
Laughter erupts, they can't comprehend,
A bowl's ambition to be a real friend!

Artisan's Lament

The potter grimaces, his hands now clay,
"Why can't I shape up this sneaky jay?"
He tosses a lump, it lands with a splat,
"On the road to glory, who knew it was that?"

"Fired!" says the kiln, a glow in his eyes,
"While I bake your blunders, do take a surprise!"
But each misfit pot gives him such glee,
"Maybe my art's not what they want to see."

Stories in the Soil

A garden's secret in every clay pot,
"Did you hear the beans gossip, oh so hot?"
Daisies chuckle, "We saw them rebel,
Telling tales of the worms, right from their shell!"

Compost murmurs, "I have seen it all,
From seedlings raising ruckus to autumn's fall."
Roots twist in laughter, sharing a jest,
"Why didn't the leaf ever take a rest?"

Rhapsodies in Earth

In the garden, pots go tumbling,
Giggling flowers, always mumbling.
A clay man with a crooked grin,
Says, "Hey, where's my leg been?"

Little frogs in custom boots,
Dancing wildly, chasing roots.
A snail slides by with a hat too large,
Declaring proudly, "I'm in charge!"

Whimsical shapes, a jester's delight,
They throw a party every night.
Mirthful laughter, the earthen clay,
Bouncing joy in a comical way.

As the sun sets, they freeze in play,
Awaiting dawn to start the fray.
Earthy tales, a silly cheer,
Who knew mud could bring such cheer?

Symbolic Shapes

A teapot shaped like a dancing bear,
Pouring tea with a well-placed flair.
Everyone laughs, what a sight to see,
When it spills and dances on the knee!

A cup with ears joins in the fun,
Grinning wide, it's never done.
It tells stories of people unnamed,
From a time when ducks were untamed.

A vase with patterns, swirling round,
Cracks a joke without a sound.
The flowers giggle, quite absurd,
An interpretation yet unheard.

They gather round in bright parade,
Sing and twirl in this joyous trade.
Shapes of mud in a playful heap,
Whimsy painted in a leap.

The Rhythm of the Form

A pot with a rhythm, beats like a drum,
With every potter's slap, more fun!
It shakes and jiggles left and right,
Declaring, "Look at my dance tonight!"

A plate that spins with a twisty shake,
Makes all the cutlery start to quake.
Forks and spoons join in with glee,
"Come on, let's mold our destiny!"

A jug that wobbles, a quirky move,
Encourages others to get in the groove.
"Let's all roll, let's all sway,
In this fabulous, muddy ballet!"

Laughter echoes in earthen song,
A rhythm of forms, where all belong.
Crafting stories from clays so pure,
In this dance, we're all secure.

Archaeology of Art

In the old dust, peculiar finds,
A soup bowl with some curious winds.
It whispers tales from dinner time,
With each splatter, there's a rhyme.

A shard of pottery, cracked yet grand,
Cup of coffee from a childish hand.
A relic with a funny note,
"Keep it hot, or I'll just float!"

Statues pose with a wink and grin,
While digging up long-lost kin.
Paleontologists rolling in glee,
Wondering who they used to be.

Unearthed laughter from ages past,
This ancient culture never cast.
Molding memories, with humor rife,
In the archaeology of our life.

Ancient Echoes

In a land where pots do sing,
Old mugs boast of everything.
A vase tried to dance, fell flat,
Now it's a shelf for a fat cat.

Digging deep to find a spoon,
A pitcher shouted, 'A festive tune!'
But all it got was a dusty look,
And a laugh from a forgotten book.

Clayborn Legends

Once a bowl dreamed of a plate,
'If I was round, I'd be first-rate!'
Nearby, a jug gave a sly wink,
'You might just end up full of drink.'

A cup claimed it brewed the best tea,
While dancing with a ceramic bee.
But all it brewed was a funny smell,
Now it's the joke of the pottery shell.

Unearthed Narratives

Found a shard with a silly grin,
It laughed loud as it joined the bin.
'We're the remnants of party nights,
Too wild for the brilliant sights!'

A teapot whispered, 'I once was gold,
Now I'm just a story told.'
And from a bowl, a voice replied,
'At least you're not the one who dried!'

Alchemy of the Artisan

A sculptor's hands knew how to play,
With mud that giggled all the way.
A turtle pot grinned, 'I'm too slow!'
While a rabbit mug stole the show.

Clays of laughter fill the shop,
Even the tiles can't help but hop.
As pottery sings in colorful tones,
We bond over our earthen bones.

The Chronicles of Fired Earth

In the kiln where laughter's born,
A potter lost his lucky horn.
He shaped a mug with a silly face,
Now it giggles in its place.

The clay just loves to tell a joke,
A teapot's laugh makes all folks choke.
With every whim, a whimsy twist,
In fired earth, no joy is missed.

Sun-Kissed Sculptures

Under the sun, the statues grin,
A chicken danced with a big ol' pin.
With shades on, they strike a pose,
Imitating the farmer's nose.

Sunbaked figures with silly hats,
A rabbit juggles all the bats.
Each curve and line has jokes to share,
In a gallery that spills with flair.

Buried Histories

Digging deep where secrets lie,
A pot of beans caught the archaeologist's eye.
He found a statue with googly eyes,
Now it keeps watch while the world sighs.

Old relics whisper tales quite absurd,
Of kings who sang, and queens who heard.
With every scoop, a giggle found,
In the dirt, where laughter's crowned.

The Embrace of Terra

A clay figure, warm and round,
Fell in love with the local ground.
With wobbly legs, it took a dance,
Tripped on roots, oh what a chance!

Embracing mud, it spun and twirled,
Made all the trees soon feel unfurled.
In a dance-off with the local breeze,
Who will win? The ground or tease?

Layers of Legacy

Once a potter made a cup,
With layers thick as grandma's fluff,
Each one told of a silly deed,
Like how he tripped while planting seed.

His pots danced on the crafty shelf,
Confessing tales of their own self,
One claimed it held a magic brew,
But spilled its secrets, oh so true.

Cups wiggled, laughed in bright array,
Joined the table in a potter's play,
They sang of clay and earthy fun,
Not one was serious, not one.

At night they whispered, loud as drums,
Of cracking jokes and playful thumbs,
Legacy in every glaze,
A legacy of joy always stays.

The Pulse of Porcelain

In the heart of the studio, a rush,
A porcelain vase got in a hush,
It claimed to have the fastest beat,
But it's just full of leftovers to eat.

Jugs and bowls held secret fights,
Over who had the funniest sights,
One said, "I held soup, oh so grand!"
While another said, "I'm just a weird band!"

Later in the kiln, they blurted out,
Toasty tales filled with laughter and doubt,
Each firing a giggle, a sly little mirth,
They pulsed with joy, for all they were worth.

And so their stories twirled like smoke,
A comedy of clays, with every poke,
Porcelain's rhythm, a jolly affair,
A beat that keeps us laughing everywhere.

Kilnside Reveries

At the kiln, where potters dream,
Sat a turtle, or so it seemed,
He tried to be the first to bake,
But ended up in a silly shake.

Mugs joked about their painted grins,
While claiming each had the best sins,
One claimed it danced at the fair,
Another said, "But I'm just a chair!"

So they spun tales round and round,
Of pots who tripped and hugs profound,
It's all a game of merry clay,
Where every piece has something to say.

As the kiln chimed, their laughter rang,
Echoing tales like a fun-filled slang,
As dreams of firing grew wild and free,
Each kilnside reverie was pure glee.

Narrative in Neolithic

In ancient days when clay was king,
There lived a bowl with quite a fling,
It claimed to hold the latest gossip,
But everyone knew it was just a tip.

Clay figures giggled at the press,
Saying, "We're a pretty good mess!"
One said, "I've got a broken grip,"
As another pirouetted with a slip.

Together they formed a jolly bunch,
Creating dishes for a funky lunch,
Other pots swayed to a playful tune,
In the firelight, they'd boogie and swoon.

Neolithic laughs echo through time,
In every crack, there's a punchline rhyme,
From silly spills to playful shapes,
The legacy of laughter escapes.

Eloquent Earth

In my garden, pots of clay,
Dancing reeds begin to sway.
A gnome with a mischievous grin,
Steals my hat and wears it thin.

The flowers laugh, they wiggle tight,
In the moon's soft, silver light.
Squirrels gossip, trees do sing,
Every earthen jar's a king!

Palaces made of mud and stone,
Kings and queens made all alone.
Who knew dirt could wear a crown?
In this world, no need to frown!

And every shard that cracks and breaks,
Tells a story with wild stakes.
So let's toast our fancy pots,
To the laughter life begot!

Once Upon a Vase

Once there lived a silly vase,
Wobbly legs, a clumsy face.
He tripped on air, he fell on grass,
Spilling water, what a mess!

The daisies giggled, oh what fun,
While bees buzzed 'round in the sun.
Chasing joy in every crack,
Oh, this vase will never lack!

One day a cat came by to play,
With paws so soft, it spun away.
A dance began, a crazy whirl,
This clay pot had a twirl!

Now they frolic, best of friends,
The vase and cat, what joy it sends.
With every crack, comes laughter bright,
In their garden of delight!

Echoes of Hand and Heart

With sticky hands and clay on feet,
I molded dreams that can't be beat.
A pot that sings and dances too,
If only it had a sense of hue!

The laughter echoes through the lane,
As my creations share their pain.
A bowl that trips and tries to flee,
From all the spills of crumply tea!

Handmade hearts with silly grins,
Awaiting hugs from all their kin.
The more they laugh, the more they crack,
It's a joy-filled, mud-slinging track!

In this place, we shape our fate,
With laughter, love, it's never late.
So come along, let's craft and play,
In echoes bright, we'll find our way!

The Heart of Clay

Once a heart, made from the earth,
Tumbled down, it found its worth.
It cracked a smile, it wore a frown,
And danced around like a silly clown.

It met a dish, quite round and bold,
Who shared its dreams and tales untold.
They laughed at pots that spilled their drink,
Bubbling over with joyous wink!

Friends with each bump, friends with each drop,
Their friendship never seemed to stop.
Together they spun in the sun,
Two merry hearts, just having fun!

So let's create with all we've got,
In this clay world, we'll hit the spot.
With every mold, we bring the cheer,
In the heart of clay, we've nothing to fear!

Dreams in Dust

In a village where pots dance with glee,
Everyone knows the clay talks for free.
Each shape a secret, a tale to unfold,
Laughter escapes from the ancients of old.

One day a bowl claimed to see in the night,
But tripped on a spoon, what a comical sight!
With a crack and a chip, it tumbled around,
The whole town erupted in giggles, profound.

A jug told a story of a far-off land,
But forgot the punchline, it didn't go as planned.
"Just laugh with me folks!" it exclaimed with a sigh,
Its spout dripped with laughter, oh me, oh my!

So here in this village where earthenware play,
Every clay creation brightens the day.
From pots full of laughter to vases so bold,
They'll share their funny tales until they grow old.

Fables of the Fired Earth

Once lived a dish who dreamed of the sea,
It yearned for a life far from cups of tea.
"I'll sail on the waves!" it declared with a cheer,
Till it wobbled and wiggled, then fell in the rear.

A teapot once boasted, "I brew the best cuppa!"
Yet spilled all its tea with a clumsy flumpa.
The villagers giggled, no tea was to share,
"Let's toast to our friend, who's beyond a repair!"

A saucer quipped wise, "Don't judge by a spill,
For laughter's the key, not just drinking your fill."
So they danced 'round the fire, with smiles all aglow,
In a realm where the fired jesters always show.

The Artisan's Hand

An artisan molded a cat with a hat,
But it slipped off its head and went splat!
"Oh dear!" cried the potter, "What a funny sight!"
The cat grinned and laughed, "I feel so light!"

With every mishap, new forms came to be,
A fish wore a scarf, oh what a spree!
They held a parade down the cobbled street,
Where pots and pans danced, a whimsical feat.

A bird in a bowl sang the tunes of the day,
With tricks up its sleeve, it led on the way.
Shaping the laughter like molding the clay,
In a world where humor would always hold sway.

Imprints of Identity

A plate had a mark that looked just like me,
With squiggly lines that made folks all tee-hee!
"Look here!" it proclaimed, "I'm the jester of plates!"
And danced on the table, oh, what crazy fates.

A mug claimed it held the best coffee of all,
But spilled it on Dad, causing quite the brawl.
"Oops!" it did chuckle, as Dad wiped his face,
While everyone laughed at the brewing disgrace.

In this land of fingerprints and quirky designs,
Every pot holds a laugh, as life intertwines.
In clay we find comfort, and in joy, we connect,
Cultivating humor with every perfect defect.

Echoes from the Kiln

In the kiln where secrets hide,
Laughter dances, pots collide.
With every crack and joyful cheer,
Clay figures smile, best friends here.

A squirrel snuck in, thought it was sweet,
To nibble on a cup, his favorite treat!
But the cup yelled, 'Hey, I'm for tea!'
The squirrel ran off, didn't agree.

Firing tempers reach the sky,
As pots debate who's the best pie.
'I'm the bowl! I hold the stew!'
'Well, I'm the plate! Who's serving you?'

With hands of clay, we shape and mold,
Crafting tales both silly and bold.
In the kiln of humor, we find our cheer,
Echoes of laughter, we hold so dear.

Vessels of Voice

A teapot sings of morning's glee,
While plates gossip about the tea.
'What's that noise?' the mugs inquire,
'I think it's the kettle on fire!'

Pans parade with pot lids clanging,
Dance across the shelf, they're hanging.
'Who brings the spice? It's my turn now!'
'You're too salty, take a bow!'

Cereal bowls chuckle, 'Look at us!'
They're filled with stories, never a fuss.
'Last week, I held a fruity jam!'
'And I had cornflakes, yum, oh ma'am!'

In this raucous kitchen flair,
The vessels chat without a care.
With clay and laughter, we all rejoice,
Together we are, Vessels of Voice!

Stories in the Soil

In the ground where wonders lie,
Clay creatures dream and give a sigh.
'Tell me a tale from long ago,'
A snail requests, 'Let's take it slow!'

A worm boasts of the things he's seen,
In gardens lush and fields of green.
'I met a beetle, oh what a sight!'
They both giggle, 'What a delight!'

Rabbits hop with twinkling eyes,
'We've heard of a pot that can fly!'
But underneath, they dig and delve,
Creating worlds they can't quite shelve.

In the soil, stories sprout and twirl,
Every nook hides a tiny pearl.
With laughter and dreams, from roots we grow,
Telling our tales, in soil we sow.

The Mosaic of Mortar

In a world where colors blend,
Mortar meets clay, on them we depend.
A wall of giggles, bricks in a line,
Painting our lives, so bright and fine.

One brick told a joke so sly,
The others cracked up, 'Oh my, oh my!'
With colors like rainbows, they're proud to be,
A mosaic of stories, wild and free.

Each chip and chip, it holds a tale,
From a clumsy builder who'd often fail.
But with laughter and grit, he made it right,
Creating a castle that sparkles bright.

In the mortar's mix, joy takes flight,
A patchwork of laughter, a joyful sight.
With every piece and every laugh,
A home of stories, our glowing path.

The Language of Loam

In a field of dreams, I found a pot,
A dancing clay man, who tells me a lot.
He wobbles and giggles, he spins around,
With every small twist, new charms will abound.

The sun shines bright on his silly face,
Waving at bugs, with such a big grace.
He whispers to flowers, they answer in cheer,
It's quite the odd sight, but I can't interfere.

His legs are quite short, his arms are too long,
With such an odd body, he sways to a song.
The wind is his partner, they twirl with delight,
As dirt flies around, oh, what a funny sight!

So if you're alone, and need some fun,
Just dig in the earth, go out for a run.
You might meet a friend, made of mud and of mirth,
And explore the great joys of this silly earth.

Whispers of the Wheel

Once on a wheel, with a spin and a twirl,
I created a bowl that looked like a curl.
It tipped and it flopped, then wobbled with glee,
Chasing my dreams, as clumsy as me.

My clay began talking, saying 'What a mess,'
It wiggled and giggled, avoiding the stress.
I tried to be serious, to make a grand vase,
But it laughed so hard, I just laughed in disgrace.

With each little swirl, it entwined a new tale,
Of flying potters, and pots that set sail.
A laughter erupted, filling the room,
As I made a clay butterfly that went 'zoom!'

So if you grab clay, don't fret if it's shy,
Just let it have fun, and give it a try.
The wheel spins on, and laughter will swell,
In a world of clay, there's always a spell.

Chiseled in Time

I chiseled a statue, with a grin quite absurd,
With a nose like a pickle, and wings of a bird.
He posed with a wink, struck a comical feat,
Declared he'd be king, while balancing on feet.

With a hammer I tapped, and he bounced with glee,
Laughing so hard, he just stopped being me.
His body was stout, but oh what a face!
He danced with the dust, in a wild, funny space.

The villagers came, said, "What's this design?"
"It's art!" I proclaimed, "Just drink some good wine."
But with every toast, he wobbled and swayed,
Soon my chiseled king, was cleverly played.

So let's carve some joy, let our spirits take flight,
In the funny and whimsical, we find pure delight.
We carve out our laughter, our joys left unwound,
In the silly of life, true treasure is found.

Memories in Malleable Earth

In a garden of clay, where giggles can rise,
I molded a monster with enormous eyes.
He blinked and he burped, rolled over with cheer,
Said, "Being made of muck, I've nothing to fear!"

He swaggered on over, with clay-covered toes,
Chasing after mushrooms, and tumbling with crows.
"Let's dance," he declared, and he twirled in the mud,
Splattering laughter, in a huge, happy flood.

With every squelch, he let out a roar,
Of memories made in a joyous uproar.
We squished and we played, with the earth all around,
In the funny old world, our happiness found.

So remember, dear friend, when your worries grow tight,
Just shape a new monster, and dance in the light.
In the silliness crafted from memories dear,
The joy we create, will always be near.

Molded by History

In a village, pots do dance,
With each splash, they take a chance.
Jugs with faces, pots with glee,
They gossip softly, oh, can't you see?

Cat's paw prints leave a mark,
On clay mounds, in daylight spark.
Grandma's secret recipe,
For potluck laughs, oh so free!

A baker's dozen, but wait, what's this?
A saucer spins, a mug asks for bliss.
Between giggles and playful cheers,
Pots share tales of ancient years.

With a whir and a twirl, they stand,
Swaying gently, hand in hand.
History's molded humor shines,
In every crack, a story aligns.

Impressions of a Maker

Lump of clay, such shy delight,
From fingertips, it takes to flight.
Swirls and curls, oh what a show,
One little nudge, and away they'll go!

A bowl that winks, a cup with charm,
Pots giggle softly, no need for alarm.
A cat jumps in, what a surprise,
With slippery paws, it tries to rise.

Stomp, stomp, squish and squabble,
Through the mud, the makers hobble.
Fresh impressions in the sun,
As laughter draws, the clay is fun.

Mold it quick, and mold it fine,
A dance of hands, a secret sign.
Their maker grins, with glee in tow,
As each piece shouts, "Look, here I glow!"

Fired by Passion

Underneath the fiery glow,
Pots are singing, stealing the show.
Sizzles, pops, and clinks of cheer,
A kiln's rave party, come gather near!

Fractured dreams in shards of clay,
They laugh and giggle, come what may.
A mug dreams of coffee, hot and bold,
While a vase dreams of flowers, daring and gold.

Heat and fire, a potter's kiss,
Forms meld together—what pure bliss!
An artist stumbles, oops, oh dear!
A broken piece now shifts the cheer.

But out they come, all gleaming bright,
Dancing pots in the soft moonlight.
Fired by passion, raw and true,
Each piece shines, a vibrant view!

The Return to the Earth

Buried deep, a fragment lies,
Once a vessel of laughter and cries.
In a garden where wildflowers dance,
Molded clay finds its second chance.

Whiskered rabbits hopping by,
Admire the shards, oh my, oh my!
In the soil, stories seep,
Pots chuckle softly, secrets to keep.

Roots embrace with gentle care,
Stroking clay, a love affair.
Nature's whims make stories new,
In every rustle, a tale rings true.

And when the rain begins to fall,
Pots sing a tune, a charming call.
With each drop, they wink and twirl,
In muddy joy, they dance and swirl!

Echoes of the Materia

In a village where jokes are quite grand,
Lived a potter who forgot where he'd stand.
His bowls flew away, oh what a sight,
Chasing clay dishes that danced in the night.

With a roll and a thud they bounced down the lane,
Causing laughter and causing some pain.
The townsfolk would giggle and point with delight,
As pots played the hero in their funny plight.

A cup took a tumble, his handle went snap,
He rolled with a chuckle, a comical rap.
"There's no use in fretting," he'd grin while he spun,
"For each broken piece, I've still got my fun!"

From jars that would jump to mugs that would sing,
He'd craft all their tales, like a funny spring.
As echoes of laughter filled up the whole square,
The clay had them rolling, no room for despair.

Resilient Red

In a land where the sun shined bright and bold,
A clay pot named Red was a sight to behold.
With a smile on his rim, he'd dance in the breeze,
Spinning tales of mischief with shimmy and tease.

One day he took flight on a flimsy kite,
Daring the wind to give him a fright.
But alas, the string tangled, he soared much too high,
And the children all laughed watching Red touch the sky.

He twirled with the clouds, feeling quite grand,
Till he landed — plop! — on an unsuspecting hand.
"Who throws a pot?" was the cry in the crowd,
But Red just chuckled, he was smug and proud.

For in every fall, he found joy in the game,
Resilient and red, he'd never be tame.
With a glint in his glaze and a chip in his side,
He wore every bruise like a badge of high pride.

Threads of Tradition

In a village of weavers where laughter prevails,
A potter would spin yarns that told funny tales.
With a slip of a hand, he mixed craft with glee,
Creating fine pottery for all to see.

His jars had their whims and their stories to share,
A vase with a wig, oh, they'd comb through the hair!
"The thread of our culture is tangled and bright,
Each loop tells a tale, let's laugh through the night!"

A teapot with glasses proclaimed he could see,
The future of ceramics, as bold as could be.
As cups cracked a joke about brewing their fate,
The punchline was served well before it was late.

With each twist and turn, the craft came alive,
The threads of tradition made mischief thrive.
"We're turning the tables!" the clays all would cheer,
As laughter unraveled, the fun filled the year.

Textures of Time

In a studio bright, with textures galore,
A potter had treasures from ceiling to floor.
Each piece held a memory, some funny, some sad,
But together they whispered, and oh, what a fad!

A mug with a squint said, "I saw it all done!
From breakfast to chaos, oh boy, was it fun!"
A plate chipped a tooth while recounting a feast,
Their colorful stories never ceased in the least.

When a bowl got a wedgie that was quite absurd,
He learned to hustle and wriggle, undeterred.
"Oh bother!" he laughed, "This clay can't keep still,"
"Let's dance through the ages, with giggles we will!"

With textures of laughter, they shaped every day,
In this happy realm where the silly could play.
Each crack, every chip, brought a smile left behind,
In a world made of laughter, you'll find joy, well-defined.

The Craft of Kin

With muddy hands and clay on face,
A family fun-filled, joyful space.
Laughter erupts like bubbles in air,
As pottery wobbles, oh what a scare!

The wheel spins round, a dizzying sight,
A potting disaster, oh what a fright!
Uncle Fred's vase, a lopsided smile,
We'll laugh at this art for quite a while!

Hands patting clay, a slippery dance,
We mold and shape with childlike chance.
Each piece a treasure, or maybe not,
But our hearts are full, and that's what we've got!

At the end of the day, we gather 'round,
Admiring creations that somehow astound.
Each funny mishap, an heirloom in mind,
The true craft of kin, laughter entwined.

Resilient Relics

In dusty corners, they stand so proud,
Old pots and pans, gathering a crowd.
A teapot with cracks—a winking wink,
Are they treasures or just kitchen sink?

Grandma's old vase with its one funny ear,
Claiming to hold all our laughter and cheer.
It may be chipped, yet it stands so tall,
Holding the stories of each family brawl!

Each relic a story, a laugh or a cry,
With each little flaw, we wave memories by.
Like that mug with a handle, quite bent in the night,
Reminding us all of a very sweet bite!

In finders' keepers or misplaces of time,
These quirky pieces each have their own rhyme.
We'll treasure them dearly, our resilient crew,
Each pot tells a tale, some funny and true!

Fired Fantasies

In a kiln of dreams where chaos ignites,
We shape our wishes, and even our fights.
A bowl that says 'I like pizza' and fries,
While a mug proclaims 'I can't even' sighs!

The clay comes alive with our giggles and grins,
As we fashion our hopes like oversized pins.
My friend made a dragon, it looks like a frog,
Why is crafting so hard? I'll just blame the fog!

Each piece a laughter, each sculpture a quirk,
In the land of the fired, who's being a jerk?
With burnt edges, we cheer, it's a masterpiece,
Fired fantasies blaze, let the fun never cease!

So let's pile the clay, and let's make a scene,
Where laughter is loud, and the art's never mean.
With every slight wobble or pop as they bake,
Our whims come alive, all for art's funny sake!

Riverbeds of Reverie

By the riverside, we dig and we play,
Turning stones into treasures by the end of the day.
A shard of old pottery, what could it say?
This riverbed joke has its own witty sway!

We find a lost mug, now covered in dirt,
With a handle that looks like a little bent skirt.
"Is it valuable?" we ponder and muse,
But the laughter we share is the best kind of use!

Wading through waters, we splash and we shout,
Each bubbling discovery ignites joyful doubt.
A fish joins our fun, can you believe it's true?
This riverbed comedy is our favorite view!

With each passing wave, our giggles abound,
Each tale of the river, joyfully found.
So let's keep on laughing, in mud let's make marks,
In our riverbed dreams, we're all silly sparks!

Crafting Narratives

With hands so muddy, stories arise,
Lumpy figures wearing silly smiles.
A pinch of humor, a dash of clay,
In my workshop, fun leads the play.

Each curve and contour tells a jest,
A vase that giggles, never at rest.
A teapot winks at the coffee mug,
Oh, the laughter in this earthy hug!

Moulding characters, oh what a sight,
Funky creatures, a true delight.
An owl with glasses, a cat so sly,
In this thick soil, imagination flies!

So gather 'round for a potter's spree,
Where every pot sings in glee.
Crafting tales in colors so bright,
A whimsical world, oh what a sight!

The Muse of the Mould

In a workshop filled with so much glee,
The moulds come alive, just wait and see!
A dancing doughnut, a juggling cup,
Who knew that clay could turn up and strut?

The muse spins around, a whirlwind of fun,
She cracks jokes with pots as the day's begun.
"Be careful now!" shouts a wise old jug,
"Or you'll end up in the clay bog snug!"

A bowl with sass, a pitcher with spice,
Every creation is fancifully nice.
Go ahead, give that slab a spin,
Here in this chaos, everyone's a win!

So let the laughter flow like the clay,
With each silly piece, we mold our play.
Embrace the mess, come enjoy the trend,
In the musings of moulds, we all transcend!

Clayborne Memories

In corners dusty, treasures hide,
Clayborne memories with joy inside.
A mug with a grin, a plate that hums,
Each piece a story, the laughter comes!

An elephant dances, legs all akimbo,
While a teacup whispers, "Let's go on a limbo!"
With every twist, a new tale we weave,
In this quirky place, we learn to believe.

Clay snickers boldly, as pots do cheer,
Every mishap turns into good cheer.
A turtle triumphs, slow but so true,
In the land of make-believe, we all grew!

So let's share our secrets, our giggles galore,
With memories crafted, we always want more.
In every fired smile, let's find the key,
These clayborne tales set our laughter free!

Hands of the Ancients

With hands of the ancients, wisdom unfolds,
Muddy and happy, a sight to behold.
They shaped the stories we now exalt,
Each flick of the wrist, an ancient vault.

Fishy-faced mugs with cheeks so round,
Whispering secrets from the buried ground.
Jugs that croon in a clay-filled tune,
Echoing laughter from ancient June.

Tumbling together, they dance in the sun,
These hands from the past never cease to have fun.
"Don't drop me now!" the vase takes a bow,
As laughter echoes, here and there and how!

So raise a toast with your finest cup,
To the hands of the ancients, we all sup.
In this merry chaos, we laugh and play,
Creating clay legends, come join the fray!

The Pottery's Promise

In a world of clay and dreams,
Where cups conspire with gleams,
A pot once whispered a joke,
And cracked up 'til it broke.

A vase tripped over a shelf,
Said, "Guess I'm a bit too stealth!"
With every slip and slide,
They laughed at their curious pride.

Bowls laughed at their own fate,
"Don't blame us! We're just great!"
Each tumble brought them cheer,
In the town of pottery beer!

So here's to life in mud,
Where every fall's a flood,
Raise a cup—oh, what a joy!
To clay, our silly toy!

Masks of the Earth

A quirky mask once said,
"I wear your face instead!"
Grinning wide with clayy cheer,
It tickled all who drew near.

A lion mask growled with glee,
"Let's go chase a bumblebee!"
The bee buzzed, danced, and spun,
While the crowd laughed—oh, what fun!

A jester mask made of clay,
Joked, "I'm just here to play!"
Each giggle caused a snap,
As they bounced into a clap!

In the night light's glow and trance,
Masks began to find their dance,
So join this wild, wacky race,
With every grin, a friendly face!

Sculpting Stories

In a workshop filled with glee,
A sculptor said, "Look at me!"
With every pull and swipe of clay,
Stories danced in bright array.

A statue of a cat sat tall,
Said, "I'm royalty after all!"
But slipped on glaze, oh dear me!
Broke into a giggling spree!

A warrior gave a mighty pose,
Sneezed hard—oh, how the clay goes!
With every sculpting twist and bend,
Laughter echoed—joy without end!

So mold your dreams, don't be shy,
In every chip, a giggle nigh,
For every craftsman knows their fate,
Is joy in jest, just let it rate!

Fireside Fables

Gather 'round, here's the tale,
Of mugs who sailed on a rail!
With a teapot navigating waves,
Whistling songs of all the braves.

A cup said, "I'm on a spree!
Life's too short; let's brew some tea!"
As they danced close to the flame,
A clay pot chuckled at the game.

With a swirl and twirl so bold,
They spun stories, bright and gold,
Fireside fables cracked a grin,
With every laugh, the warmth flowed in!

So stack those tales that rise and fall,
Even mugs can have a ball,
Around the fire, let joy ignite,
With every sip, a giggly night!

In the Hands of Time

In a potter's shop, things go awry,
A cup with legs tried to fly.
It tripped on a saucer, fell with a clank,
Now it's a vase saved by a prank.

A teapot sighed, 'I'm too hot to brew!'
A kettle spooned in, 'Let's sip some dew.'
They laughed at the mugs with the grumpy face,
Who couldn't dance in their awkward space.

The bowls had a feast, while plates made a scene,
A salad bowl strutted, feeling quite keen.
All joined the fun, with no time for frowns,
In a world made of laughter, no one wears crowns.

So here's to the clay, that bends with a grin,
A world of whimsy, let the laughter begin!
No worries of gravity or pots that might break,
Just fun in the air, for goodness' sake!

Whispers of the Ancient

In a dusty old kiln, secrets fly,
Earthen whispers and laughter draw nigh.
A mug with a handle swayed to the tune,
Of a broken old jug who hummed at the moon.

The tiles had a gossip, a story to share,
Of a time they were painted with great flair.
They laughed at the vases, all stiff like a plank,
'Now look at us, we're full of spank!'

A bowl with a crack claimed, 'I'm just more wise!'
'Cracks add character!' said the old pot with pride.
As the chattering surged, they danced a fine jig,
In the cozy old shop where the stories ran big.

So let's raise a toast, with mismatched cups,
To forgotten times, to ancient hiccups.
Where laughter's the glaze that holds us together,
In a realm where the past feels light as a feather!

Tales of Mud and Fire

In the furnace, a clay blob plotted a stunt,
'Today I'll become a dazzling front!'
With a twist and a shimmy, it reached for the sky,
But ended up with a lid and a sigh.

A mug tried to whistle but sounded like rain,
A bowl just giggled, 'You're driving me insane!'
Together they dreamed of a grand pottery ball,
While catching a glimpse of a cheeky old wall.

The oven grew hot, and the pots spun around,
In the middle of chaos, a dance they had found.
They boogied and shimmied, defying their fate,
A lively soirée, and all were first-rate!

So let's sing of the clays with their wild, silly schemes,
Of laughter and dreams in their fiery dreams.
For in every crack, a fond joke surely stays,
In the tales of mud where the heart ever plays!

The Clay's Narrative

In a corner, a pot whispered slyly,
'Last week I was chosen, oh how stylishly!'
A plate with envy said, 'Now isn't that rich?
You're just a big bowl with a fancy old itch!'

A mug turned around, all spunky and bright,
'At least I am chosen to sip in delight!'
The vases were quiet, just sitting in grace,
Trying to keep a calm, dignified face.

But then came a jester, a goofy old pot,
Who danced on the shelf in a crazed little trot.
'If we're just clay, let's not take a hit,
Let's find a way to make humor a fit!'

In this merry mix, they all joined the cheer,
Creating a story that's ever so clear.
For in every swirl, every laugh, every crack,
Lies a tale that unites, no fun they'll lack!

Fired Fortunes

In the kiln we trust, our hopes alight,
With clay in hand, we mold delight.
But when it cracks, what's left to do?
We laugh and shout, "Just paint it blue!"

A cup that wobbles, a plate that spins,
Our pottery's got a case of sins.
Each artist's dream is a funny sight,
Unless it shatters in the night!

A Tapestry of Textures

From rough to smooth, a bumpy ride,
Each layer's a story, let laughs collide.
We press and roll to shape our fate,
But oops, that blob? It's just first date!

With patterns wild, and colors bright,
We craft our joys with sheer delight.
Yet when it wobbles, what can we say?
It's performance art, come join the fray!

Sculpted Dreams

With a pinch and a poke, we build our dreams,
But who knew clay had so many schemes?
With every twist, it turns to fun,
"It's a statue!" we claim, "Well, maybe just one!"

Mismatched features and a goofy grin,
Our masterpieces look like they might win.
But if they fall, don't shed a tear,
Just chuckle and say, "That's art, my dear!"

Timeworn Traditions

In the village square, we gather 'round,
With pots and pie, and laughter abound.
We tell old tales while shaping clay,
"Is it a dish or a hat?" we play!

Grandma's advice, as wise as can be,
"If it breaks, glue it! Just wait and see!"
And though our crafts may oft go awry,
We cherish the laughs, give it a try!

In the Embrace of Earth

In clay we trust, with laughter near,
Molding mischief, let's make it clear.
With sticky hands and goofy grins,
Pottery's magic, where the fun begins.

A wedged-up mess, we form a beast,
Wobbling on wheels, it looks like yeast.
Oops! It fell and cracked in two,
A lizard now, that's what it can do!

Our molded dreams, like clay in hands,
Brought to life by silly plans.
The Earth chuckles with every miss,
It's funny how we find such bliss.

So let's keep shaping, no room for doubt,
In this mud, we laugh and shout.
For every flop, a story grows,
In every piece, our joy just flows.

Strokes of Sand and Stone

With brushes made of sticks and grass,
We paint our world, let colors clash.
A canvas wild, so big and bright,
Splashes of fun in the sunny light.

Our strokes are bold, our hands a mess,
A masterpiece? Well, we guess!
The sand gets in our hair and eyes,
Still, we laugh, amid our cries.

A boulder rolls, it steals the show,
We chase it down, away we go!
Sketching lines upon the stones,
Creating joy in silly zones.

Each wink and giggle, a joyful sound,
In our art, mischief is found.
Sand and stone in a playful spree,
With each stroke, we feel so free.

Timeless Craft

In ancient hands, we spin the tale,
Of silly pots that sway and flail.
From clumsy grips and thrown-off clay,
Emerges laughter in a grand ballet.

The wheel goes round, with a giggle and swirl,
A perfect bowl? Just give it a whirl!
Our creations wobble, dance with glee,
Each twist a joke, oh can't you see?

Knocking over pots, oh what a scene,
Gooey fingers and laughter keen.
With every flop, we find a prize,
A quirky vase in goofy guise.

Timeless tricks in a playful art,
From ancient truths to modern heart.
Crafting joy with each crazy spin,
In every effort, the fun begins.

The Art of the Earth

The ground we roam is our canvas wide,
With splotchy mud, our hopes collide.
Laughter echoes through every crack,
As we get splattered, there's no turning back.

Sculpting dreams with dirt and cheer,
Stumbling around, we spin and leer.
The squirrels giggle, the birds take flight,
As we create with all our might.

A stone in hand, we carve our fate,
Each chisel laugh, we contemplate.
Mistakes become the best of friends,
In every sculpt, a story bends.

So let's dig deep, and not be shy,
With earthy crafts, we'll touch the sky.
Art of the soil, what a delight,
In every pot, our hearts ignite.

The Palette of Past.

In a village where colors dance,
The pots always wore a silly romance.
With stripes and dots all around,
These cheeky jugs laughed, sound by sound.

One jug boasted a hat made of fruit,
Another wore mismatched shoes—oh, what a hoot!
They argued who was the fanciest vase,
But in the end, each had a funny face.

The paint dripped like a rainbow rain,
Pots giggling, forgetting their pain.
"Who's breaking the clay?" one pot yelled loud,
While the rest formed a colorful crowd.

In this joyful land of terracotta beats,
Laughter echoed through the streets.
A palette of stories, oh what a blast,
With earthen jokes that forever last.

Earthen Echoes

In the heart of the clay, where laughter is spun,
The pots tell tales of silly fun.
One fell off a shelf with a clatter and crash,
And laughed the hardest, all in a flash.

With a twist and a turn, he rejoined the fray,
Shouting, "I nearly landed in yesterday!"
His friends rolled over, their sides turning red,
"All of that just for a nap on your head!"

Echoes of giggles through the garden flow,
As the pots share secrets from long ago.
"Did you hear about the lid that got stuck?"
"Oh yes, dear friend, he's out of luck!"

In earthen chambers where stories revive,
These jolly vessels keep the humor alive.
With every bump and unpolished glance,
The clay holds whispers of a merry dance.

Sculpted Whispers

In a studio where whispers frolic and play,
Sculpted pots tell tales in a quirky way.
"I was a bowl, then turned into a mug,
Now I'm a planter, oh what a rug!"

One said he was shaped like a shoe for the cat,
While another wore flowers, just imagine that!
They giggled and wobbled, a curious crew,
"In this frame of clay, what shall we do?"

Their sculpted curves sparked giggles anew,
With jokes crafted from mud and a friendly cue.
"Let's hold a party, with snacks on our rim,
And dance till the stars make the evening dim!"

Whispers of laughter on ceramic winds,
Creating a chaos where silliness begins.
In this workshop of clay where fun is designed,
Sculpted friends share joy intertwined.

Clay Dreams

In a land of dreams shaped from clay,
Pots plot pranks that will surely dismay.
One spun around with a caper so bold,
Shouting, "I'll be the hero of stories untold!"

The flower pot joked, "I want to fly high!
Tie me to a kite, let's touch the sky!"
A bowl teased back, "You'll just catch the breeze,
And land in a tree, if you please!"

Amid the clay hills where giggles unfold,
Comedic adventures and antics retold.
Each vessel had dreams of being a star,
But just landed in puddles—oh how bizarre!

In this world of clay where mirth takes the lead,
The pots dream big, planting laughter as seed.
With each wobbly step on their playful stage,
They create clay dreams filled with joy and page.

Secrets Beneath the Surface

In the clay there are whispers,
Baking under the sun's grin,
Songs of the past they murmur,
With a giggle, they begin.

Lively shapes taking a bow,
Dance in the breeze like a dream,
A frog in a hat says, "Wow!"
What a whimsical team!

Bubbles and cracks share a tale,
Of a pot that forgot how to hold,
It wobbles and tips without fail,
Seeking laughter, not gold.

Underneath secrets do hide,
In each artful, playful crack,
A laughing face, full of pride,
Hopes it won't tip and fall back.

Age-Old Colors

Colors of mischief and cheer,
Bright reds and greens that collide,
Each hue is up to some sheer,
Painting smiles they can't hide.

In a bowl that's just too round,
Cereal swims, splash looks like art,
Giggling grains dance all around,
A Picasso from the heart.

Old pots tell tales of the woe,
Of a cat that once went to town,
Paws dipped in colors, oh no!
Spent the day wearing a crown.

As the glaze dries, they all meet,
Lively laughter, a welcome cheer,
In the sun, their charms repeat,
Age-old shades that hold us near.

Voices from the Kiln

Listen close, the noise is loud,
Chirpy echoes brew and bake,
A potbellied fellow is proud,
Making sure you laugh, not quake.

Each piece emerges with a grin,
Not one that's ready to frown,
They gossip about life within,
And spin stories all around.

A coffee mug spills the tea,
About a vase that sings by night,
Saying, "Just don't spill on me!"
Join us in this silly fight.

In this hot box of surprise,
Creatures alive seem to play,
Who knew such fun could arise,
From clay that's shaped, and never gray?

Dust and Dance

In the dust, tiny feet prance,
Pots and jars find their meter,
They spin and twirl, join the dance,
With every tap, life gets sweeter.

A sprinkle of ash adds flair,
Stirring up giggles in the air,
A spoon joins in with a flair,
Creating rhythm everywhere!

Each sweep of dust tells a tale,
Of mishaps and playful delight,
When pots wobbled without fail,
And danced under the moonlight.

So come, take a laugh-filled chance,
Join the potters, take a twirl,
In the play of clay, we enhance,
With dust and dreams that whirl.

Earthbound Whimsy

In the garden, pots hold dreams,
Plants gossip by the sunlit beams.
Gnomes dance with a wink and a jest,
While weeds wear crowns, feeling blessed.

A lizard claims his ceramic throne,
Waving to squirrels, not feeling alone.
Bugs in boots tap their tiny feet,
In this clay kingdom, life's quite a treat.

Potted peas throw a playful shout,
Melting hearts with a twist and a pout.
They dream of journeys on a breeze,
But settle down for snuggles and cheese.

In this land, each pot tells a tale,
Of whimsical quests without fail.
Where laughter blooms and colors play,
In the earthy humor of a sunny day.

The Creation of Culture

A sculptor shapes with hands so grand,
Each curve whispers, 'This was planned!'
Funny figures, with noses like fries,
Strut around, much to our surprise.

Bowls and mugs boast colorful flair,
Chipping in jokes with a cheeky glare.
They trade barbs with each whirling spin,
As teapots giggle when pouring in.

In this realm of art and clay,
Each piece has something funny to say.
Urns crack jokes about their old age,
While quirky mugs take center stage.

From the wheel, stories sprout like trees,
In a playful dance with the gentle breeze.
Laughter echoes through every land,
As culture grows from a soft, warm hand.

Firing the Imagination

In the kiln, dreams get sizzled tight,
As laughter bubbles up, pure delight.
Dancing pots sizzle with glee,
In a fiery whirl of creativity.

A whale shaped vase lies there with flair,
Singing tunes of a salty air.
Wobbly bowls clap in a clay brigade,
While the oven chuckles at the parade.

With each turn, the humor ignites,
As creatures emerge in colorful sights.
Funny faces and silly hats,
Making the audience laugh like spats.

The heat crafts tales with an eager grin,
As imagination tosses thoughts within.
From the coals and bricks, stories will bloom,
With a sprinkle of joy, lighting up the room.

Shapes of Heritage

A jug tiptoes with ancient grace,
While bowls gather in a laughing race.
Old stories wrapped in quirky clay,
Dance through time in a playful sway.

A kettle spins, a circus act,
Just waiting for tea, that's a fact!
Mugs with mustaches do a dance,
Earning their place with a playful glance.

Every shape holds a history bright,
Crafted with giggles, full of delight.
Saucers sing of traditions bold,
While vases shimmer with tales of old.

Heritage laughs in each little nook,
As artifacts wink like a favorite book.
In this clay world, where stories ignite,
Shaped by humor, culture takes flight.

www.ingramcontent.com/pod-product-compliance
Lightning Source LLC
Chambersburg PA
CBHW070322120526
44590CB00017B/2782